CONTENTS

INTRODUCTION

I remember, as a small child, family reunions held each summer in a picnic grove alongside an old covered bridge. The wooden planking of the bridge floor rattled and thumped in announcement of each new arrival. We splashed about in the shallow water next to the stone walls that supported the bridge and fished for the trout that gathered in the cool shadows of the span. The more adventurous kids even climbed to the ledge of the one window in the side of the bridge and launched cannonball dives into the stream below.

On a vacation in the Amish country of south-central Pennsylvania many years later, I remember resting by the side of a covered bridge, dangling my

RIGHT: The description of an early nineteenth-century observer of covered bridges as "barns thrown across America's rivers" has some validity. There is much that is similar in the design and construction of bridges and of barns. West Arlington, Vermont

OPPOSITE: The entrances to a covered bridge are known as portals, a term which also can be used to refer to the boarded section of either end of the bridge under the roof. Woodstock, Vermont

feet in the cool waters of a different stream and munching a picnic lunch. My husband was casting a fishing lure into the pool beneath the bridge, this time for the small-mouth bass that had gathered in the depths there.

Several horse-drawn Amish buggies crossed the bridge, practically over my head, while we were there. Their motorless sounds were much different than the car-crossing sounds of my youth. It seemed that here, in the "plain" and traditional ways of the Amish, was the spirit that first created the covered bridge. It was as much a remnant of the premotorized era as were the Amish and their buggies.

Few icons of the American

landscape take us back in time to a quieter period in our history as does the covered bridge with its enduring strength and simplicity, in harmony with the countryside it continues to serve.

Following page:
The boxed-in, covered trusses that developed to protect truss joints on regular open bridges, and eventually led to covered bridges, can be seen in this photograph. *Comstock Bridge, Colchester, Connecticut*

RIGHT: The earliest covered bridges, like most structures in rural nineteenth-century America, were often not afforded the supreme luxury of a coating of paint. The boards were left to cure in the weather. *Scott Bridge, West Townshend, Vermont*

OPPOSITE: Windows on covered bridges are commonly covered themselves to shelter the critical interior timbers of the bridge from yet another potential intrusion by the elements. *Forty-five River, Fundy National Park, New Brunswick*

CHAPTER ONE

THE FIRST COVERED BRIDGES

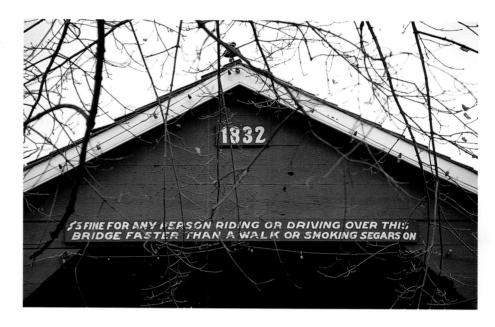

The covered bridge has not been with us nearly as long as most of us imagine in our idyllic vision of the past. It is not even as old as the United States, which was formally born on July 4, 1776. The covered bridge of America, in a version different from the one we know today, dates to the early 1800s and evolved for reasons far less romantic than we might hope.

The original idea for the covered bridge actually goes back a bit further. Its tale begins with Charles Wilson Peale, whose portrait of George Washington is today our image of the father of his country. Wanting to propel the young nation in general, and Philadelphia in particular, into a new age of prosperity, Peale elaborated on some earlier dabblings in the area of bridge construction, and designed a massive structure to span the Schuylkill River, at what is today Market Street, and open easy travel to the west of the city.

Peale's proposed bridge was a huge, arching structure that stretched 390 feet in total length. Curved truss panels would be incorporated the entire length to bring added strength to the structure.

For his efforts, on January 21, 1797, Peale received the first U.S. patent for a bridge design. He did not, however, see his bridge erected. It wasn't a covered bridge, but it set the stage for the construction of the first covered bridge.

Interest had been stirred to find a replacement for the small ferries and rickety floating bridges that still afforded the only crossings of the Schuylkill. The Schuylkill Permanent Bridge Company was formed a

The "SEGARS" reference on this covered bridge may evoke a chuckle today, but the bridge-keepers were very serious about such threats to their bridges. *South Perkasie Bridge, Bucks County, Pennsylvania*

RIGHT: The dark depths of covered bridges across the country have given rise to much folklore and many ghost stories, some originating in deaths that occurred on or near the bridges. *Frankenfield Bridge, Bucks County, Pennsylvania*

OPPOSITE: Although our familiar image of the covered bridge is much like this single-lane construction, bridges with two passages, known as double-barrel, were not uncommon during the heyday of the bridges. *Williamsburg, Vermont*

little more than a year later, on March 16, 1798, for that express purpose.

The company's bridge construction began on a course to erect an all-stone span and proceeded with that plan at a very slow and painful pace for several years without ever completing a bridge. The designer, William Weston, who by that time had left the project and returned to England, sent back a plan that would have placed a cast-iron bridge atop the piers that had been set in place. However, at that point in the development of the young nation, there were no foundries on this side of the Atlantic that could produce iron of the size required by the plan.

Instead, Judge Richard Peters, president of the company and the moving force behind the project, brought in America's preeminent wooden-bridge builder at the time, Timothy Palmer. One of his own bridge designs had followed that of Peale's through the patent office by just a few months, and he had followed up on the patent by actually building bridges.

By January 1, 1805, Palmer and his workers had the trusswork of the bridge completed to the extent that it could be opened to traffic. The bridge was 550 feet long and 42 feet wide, with three spans employing Weston's

piers and featuring two lanes for traffic. It occupied the location that Peale had originally proposed.

Palmer thought his job was drawing to a close, but not so Judge Peters. He worried that exposure to the elements of rain, sleet, and snow would attack the exposed timbers continuously, eating away at the bridge and bringing on the need for costly repairs much faster than if the wood was somehow protected. Realizing the opportunity to give increased longevity to his creation, Palmer was quick to agree to the idea of "weatherboarding and roofing" the bridge.

Owen Biddle, one of Philadelphia's leading architects, was brought in to add the sides and then top them off with a roof. He apparently realized the significance of what he had been asked to do and took elaborate pains. The lower half of each side was constructed to look like blocks of stone and even sprinkled with stone dust atop fresh paint to enhance that appearance. Large, false colonnades were placed along the sides, which also carried forty-four round windows with shutters.

EARLY AMERICAN BRIDGES

The protective aspect of covering on bridges, now given full expression, had not escaped earlier American

A Z-cut like this one provides a more secure connection, with needed room for expansion and contraction of the wood, than does a simple end-to-end connection between timbers. *Offutt's Ford Bridge, Rush County, Indiana*

The strength of the timbers used in covered bridges can almost be felt in this study of floor detail from a bridge built in 1868 over Sugar Creek. *Darlington Bridge, Montomery County, Indiana*

bridge builders. As early as the mid-1780s, builders were covering the pressure spots on their bridges, particularly those where the support timbers were joined to create longer spans than single support structures could cover.

However, long before that the very first bridges were simply trees felled across streams at points where trails crossed the water. These precarious spans were known as stringers.

Those logs provided crossings for little more than individual travelers and were soon replaced with a rough bridge design known as the corduroy.

Logs were still the material for the corduroy bridges, but now—as early as 1650—two larger, longer timbers were placed across the waterway, parallel to

one another. Smaller, split logs were laid side by side atop the two supporting timbers to form the floor along the length of the bridge. Additional split logs were attached over the floor timbers, parallel to the original supports. Where necessary, short log ramps were added at the ends of the bridge to make access a bit easier and less abrupt.

Around 1700, American bridge designers began to incorporate the concept of the truss into their constructions. A truss, one of the basic concepts of engineering, is a framework of beams—wooden at the time—arranged as a triangle from the ends of the bridge to a point above the bridge. It strengthens the overall bridge, but creates joints between timbers where additional wear-and-tear will take place.

Devices known as "ship's knees" can be seen in the braces that lead from the sides to the roof of this covered bridge. These were incorporated into the bridge to increase its rigidity. *Ashuelot Bridge, Ashuelot, New Hampshire*

OPPOSITE: Most covered bridges remaining today provide crossings over relatively small streams. A few, however, have been maintained over wide waterways. *Saco River Bridge, Conway, New Hampshire*

GALLON HOUSE BRIDGE
84 FT HOWE TRUSS SPAN
ACROSS ABIQUA CREEK
BUILT IN 1916

EXPLORATION AND EXPERIMENT

To fight off the impact of the elements on their trusses, builders by the late 1700s had created the boxed truss. In this variation after the trusses were in place on the bridge, wooden enclosures were built around them. The roof of the truss covering, known as the weather plate, was slanted to the outside of the bridge to direct the runoff away from the floor of the bridge. The result was a pair of relatively wide and hollow, triangular or multi-triangular, walls along the sides of the bridge. The floor of the bridge was still exposed to the elements, but the trusses were now covered.

The prototype of a fully covered bridge was now in place. It was just a matter of time before execution followed suggestion and most of the boxed-truss bridges were roofed over and thus converted into covered bridges.

WHY COVERED BRIDGES?

Protection of the base structure from the elements is almost certainly the primary reason behind covered bridges. It comes up again and again in those discussions that preceded bridge building and was also recorded in one format or another. However, various researchers—and covered bridges have attracted many—have turned up additional rationale in conversations with older generations.

The sides and roof not only rebuffed the destructive effects of weather on the bridge, but also kept the roadway of the bridge dry of rain and clear of snow. This was a concern of early bridge users, because the timbers were generally oiled to give them longer useful lives and could become slippery when wet.

Further, the added dimensions of sides and a roof brought greater overall strength to the bridge. And, of course, it was easier to encourage animals

The multiple kingpost truss supports this bridge. This design is but one that led to the development of covered bridges. *The Flume, Franconia Notch State Park, New Hampshire*

RIGHT: The roofs of most covered bridges were not as wide as this one, which clearly meets the need for protection from the elements that motivated the development of covered bridges. *Rowell Bridge, West Hopkinton, New Hampshire*

OPPOSITE: Pilings, such as these under the open bridge leading up to the covered bridge, were sometimes used in place of piers or abutments to support bridges where the stream bottom was uncertain. *Gallon House Bridge, Silverton, Oregon*

What eventually became widely known as the "Pennsylvania buttress" here supports each end of a two-span structure with stony strength. *Frankenfield Bridge, Bucks County, Pennsylvania*

Today we generally refer to the appearance of the lumber on this covered bridge as weather-beaten, but throughout most of America's early history it carried the much more pleasing description of "weather-cured." *Tunbridge, Vermont*

To provide for an extended roof on this covered bridge, the builder has placed additional, mini-truss structures extended from the framework of the bridge to the rafters of the roof.
Sunday River Bridge (Artist's Bridge), Newry, Maine

Though the snow lies heavy over the countryside, it is not resting on any of the bridge timbers except those of the roof. The others are protected from the damaging effects of snow and ice.
West Cornwall, Connecticut

to cross an enclosed bridge than an open one where the running water beneath can be observed. This was important at a time when the only means of locomotion was draft animals.

A CHOICE OF MATERIALS

"If you've seen one covered bridge, you've seen them all," may very well become the battle-cry of a tour-weary youngster who had very different expectations of just what a covered bridge tour would be at the start of the day. But nearly every covered bridge has a design feature or two that gives it a character all its own. This might be the plank-sided span, with just a pair of small windows at its midpoint, in a park in Allentown, Pennsylvania. Or it might be the open, lattice-like sides of the bridge over the Red Clay Creek near Ashland, Delaware. Or the two-laner at Camp Nelson, Kentucky. Or the span near Rushville, Indiana, which includes a covered pedestrian walkway on either side of the roadway.

Although it's the external appearance of the covered bridge that leaves the first and often most lasting impression, the interior beam-structure of the bridge often reveals more about its history. The simple triangular truss described earlier, known as the kingpost truss, was among the earliest advances in American bridge building. It was followed by the queenpost truss, which substituted a horizontal crosspiece in place of the triangular peak of the kingpost and thus allowed for longer spans.

The effect of covering is clear in this view from inside a covered bridge just after a rainstorm. While the roadway is wet, the floor timbers are damp only at the entrance to the bridge. *Albany Bridge, White Mountain National Forest, New Hampshire*

OPPOSITE: The slant of the roof and its weather-repellent abilities are continued in the bridge's slanted sides, a relatively recent design alteration. *Chitwood, Oregon*

CHAPTER TWO

THE MEN BEHIND THE BRIDGES

Regardless of the auspicious beginning of the covered bridge in America by widely known and popular men at the top of their professions, most of the lesser covered bridges were built by men with no renown beyond that in their local communities. The bridges over much of the American landscape were simple necessities for continued prosperity of the community and were planned and built as needed by local craftsmen.

LEWIS WERNWAG, BRIDGE BUILDER

One of those who did rise to a certain national prominence in the design of covered bridges, right alongside Palmer, was the German immigrant Lewis Wernwag. The young man was just beginning his career as a bridge-builder's apprentice when Peale's plans were earning their patent. He disdained the early covered bridges he observed, describing them as "barnlike structures that Americans are throwing across their rivers."

Wernwag got his chance to show the bridge-building fraternity a new way in 1811. Once again, a group of monied interests in Philadelphia was looking to construct yet another span across the Schuylkill River, this time at what today is the Fairmount section of the city.

Local architect Robert Mills had already completed plans for the bridge when the businessmen behind the venture decided they wanted Wernwag to lead the actual construction. Wernwag grabbed the opportunity to redesign the span to his own liking. Mills recognized the bridge builder's abilities and agreed to all his changes, as Wernwag drew up plans for an ambitious 400-foot-long bridge.

The money men behind the venture, however, were not as receptive. After much squabbling they,

The top and bottom members of a truss, clearly visible beneath this New England example, are known as chords. They can be made of a single piece of wood or several joined pieces. *Waterville, Vermont*

RIGHT: The floor beams, upon which the travel surface of the bridge is erected, are clearly visible on this single span resting securely on stone "Pennsylvania buttresses." *Slaughterhouse Bridge, Northfield, Vermont*

OPPOSITE: The Burr truss, named for one of America's pioneers in covered-bridge construction, Theodore Burr, supports this well-maintained bridge. *Valley Forge National Historical Park, Pennsylvania*

FOLLOWING PAGE: Although today we commonly associate roadways with covered bridges, there was a time in the early development of the country's railroads when wooden covered bridges carried this form of conveyance as well. *Manning Bridge, Washington*

Wernwag, and Mills agreed to a span of 300 feet in length and began work on April 8, 1812. The finished project, actually 340 feet when completed, was the second-longest, single-span covered bridge on earth. It was immediately christened "The Colossus" by local commentators, a name it carried until it burned down in 1838.

Wernwag's reputation as a bridge builder was made. He continued to build on that reputation, erecting spans in various locations throughout Pennsylvania. His base of operations was at the spot on the Schuylkill River that today is the town of Phoenixville, Pennsylvania, where he also managed an ironworks for a conglomerate of Philadelphia business interests. When after the War of 1812 a declining economy ruined the iron business, Wernwag moved to Conowingo, Maryland, along the Susquehanna River and set up a sawmill.

As the sawmill grew, Wernwag's enthusiasm for bridges began to increase. Soon the mill was turning out pre-cut bridge kits that were floated down the Susquehanna and along the Chesapeake Bay to where they were needed in coastal Maryland and Virginia. He gave up the Conowingo site in 1824, but left behind a ten-span covered bridge across the Susquehanna for the use of his potential western shore customers.

Wernwag now located his operation on Virinius

Island at the confluence of the Shenandoah and Potomac rivers, not surprisingly connected to both the Virginia and Maryland sides of the Potomac by a covered bridge.

The bridge-builder was now more of a corporation than an individual. Many of the bridges that carried his name, and his trademark flared kingpost, after this point were actually designed and built by men in Wernwag's employ, with only cursory involvement by the great man. Their work could be found as far west as Kentucky.

The "lattice mode" style of truss arrangement, a truly American creation, was developed by bridge-builder Ithiel Town. It first appeared in 1820. Erwinna Bridge, Bucks County, Pennsylvania

RIGHT: The interior of a covered bridge is an intricate array of crossing, meeting, and opposing timbers all placed with one goal in mind, supporting the bridge span and negating the effects of gravity. West Dummerstone Bridge, Vermont

OPPOSITE: The style of Lewis Wernwag, builder of the famous Colossus in Philadelphia, was marked by flared kingpost trusses combined with a huge double arch to bring added strength to the span. Scott Bridge, Townshend, Vermont

This bridge displays the boxed-X design developed and made popular in the 1820s by Colonel Stephen H. Long. *Bridge No. 37, Stark Village, New Hampshire*

The idea of adding iron rods to the truss structure of covered bridges, such as seen here on a New Hampshire bridge, was introduced in 1840 by William Howe. *Ashuelot Bridge, Ashuelot, New Hampshire*

Built in 1832, this colorful bridge features the crossing timbers design of the Long truss as well as an extension of the roof and platform for a pedestrian walkway. *Thompson Bridge, Swanzey, New Hampshire*

When covered bridges were the primary means of conveyance, travelers were strictly regulated in order to protect the structures, since often they were constructed and maintained at significant cost to the community. *Cornish-Windsor Bridge, Cornish, New Hampshire*

THE MOST PROLIFIC
COVERED-BRIDGE BUILDER

A third great innovator in the early days of the American covered bridge was Theodore Burr, whose Burr truss represented yet another advancement in the technology of bridge support. Within each side of the covered bridge, Burr constructed a large arch between two kingposts. The design, patented in 1804, allowed for a level floor to the bridge, even over considerable spans.

The longest single-span covered bridge using the Burr truss was 360 feet, which also was the longest single-span wooden bridge ever built. It crossed the Susquehanna River at McCall's Ferry, Pennsylvania. Completed in 1815, the bridge was broken to bits and carried away by an ice jam of historic proportions in March 1818.

Burr began his bridge-building career in New York, but after just a few years moved to Pennsylvania, which was the center of development for early

The first panel at the end of the truss on each side of a covered bridge is known as the shelter panel. Its boarding protects the timbers of the truss from moisture blowing into the portals. *Imes Bridge, St. Charles, Iowa*

OPPOSITE: Sheet metal roofs are a relatively recent addition to American covered bridges. In the construction of earlier examples, wood was the only material readily available to the builders. *Staats Mill Bridge, Jackson County, West Virginia*

covered-bridge construction. His instincts proved accurate when he landed state-government contracts to build three of four new bridges across the Susquehanna River. At one point he had bridges under construction at Northumberland, Harrisburg, and, of course, McCall's Ferry.

It was Burr's Harrisburg bridge that Charles Dickens described in a much-quoted entry in his travel journal of an 1842 tour of America.

"We crossed the river by a wooden bridge, roofed and covered on all sides, and nearly a mile in length. It was profoundly dark; perplexed with great beams, crossing and recrossing it at every possible angle; and through the broad chinks and crevices in the floor, the rapid river gleamed, far down below, like a legion of eyes. We had not lamps; and as the horses stumbled and floundered through this place, toward the distant speck of dying light, it seemed interminable.

"I really could not at first persuade myself as we rumbled heavily on, filling the bridge with hollow noises, and I held down my head to save it from the rafters above, but that I was in a painful dream; for I had often dreamed of toiling through such places, and as often argued, even at the time, 'This cannot be reality.'"

By the time he died in 1822, at age fifty-one, Burr had personally designed and directed the construction of nearly fifty bridges. His designs and ideas were copied on an untold number of other bridges throughout the growing nation. So widely known was the bridge builder that by the time his bridges were being copied in the western frontier they often were referred to as "burrs."

But Burr never really benefited financially from all his innovations and energies. He died without sufficient funds for a burial, while working on a small bridge over the Swatara Creek in Middletown, Pennsylvania,

and was buried without a marker. The location of the resting spot of the most prolific bridge builder of his time has been lost to time.

YANKEE INGENUITY

The fourth contract on the Susquehanna River went to Jonathan Walcott, a Connecticut bridge builder who like Burr had come to Pennsylvania to get in on the frenzy in span construction, and Pennsylvania carpenters Henry and Samuel Slaymaker. Their bridge, at Columbia, Pennsylvania, was the longest covered bridge ever built with wood. Its 5,690-foot span (410 feet longer than a mile) was supported atop twenty-eight stone piers.

Another Connecticut builder, Ithiel Town, was one of the first of America's bridge builders to earn a comfortable living from his ideas. His Town Lattice-Truss design, which employed a series of diagonally opposing beams along both sides of the bridge, was patented in early 1820. He immediately capitalized on that patent by selling rights to its use for the sum of $1 per foot of bridge. Because Town's design allowed the framework of a bridge to be constructed of much shorter timbers than was the general practice of the day many were ready to pay that dollar, both in America and in Europe.

Although the original stone masonry of the parapets of this covered bridge remain intact at the far end of bridge, their contemporary piers in the stream have been subsequently replaced with modern concrete. *Stark Village, New Hampshire*

OPPOSITE: Relatively modern truss techniques can be seen in this covered bridge, which was erected in 1936. *Eureka, California*

A double-barreled bridge, very rare today, features separate passageways for two lanes of traffic, in this case oncoming motor vehicles. *Brown County State Park, Nashville, Indiana*

The addition of iron rods to the truss of the covered bridge signaled a new era in the history of covered bridges in America, the point at which railroads began to spread across the land. *Roann Bridge, Wabash County, Indiana*

The basic gable-style roof, also common on American barns, was the most common roof design used for covered bridges across the country. It was simple and functional. *Bollinger Mill State Historical Site, Burfordville, Missouri*

Joining a wooden bridge to a stone foundation created spaces where water could collect. Special measures, such as curved siding or small gable roofs over stone pieces, were used to deflect run-off. *Bureau Creek Bridge, Bureau County, Illinois*

RAILROADS TAKE CENTER STAGE

William Howe from Massachusetts brought iron to the bridge-building process. Following the crossed-beam truss design that Colonel Stephen Long had developed in 1829 and improved during the 1830s, for which the emerging railroads had already shown a preference, Howe added iron rods in critical tension spots.

Long was working for the Baltimore & Ohio Railroad (B&O) when he created his namesake truss to carry America's first overpass. It was one of the first covered bridges employed by the railroads, but it did not carry a railroad at all. It lifted a surface road—the Washington Pike—over the railroad bed.

The Colonel's Yankee frugality was his primary motivation for designing the bridge, named the Jackson Bridge for the then-president of the United States. Total cost was just $1,670 and total time of construction was only seven and a half weeks. These features, Long was convinced, were critical to the swift advancement of the United States to the west. To that end he spent a great deal of money and energy promoting his innovations.

As the railroads continued that westward march they

One of the earliest truss designs to emerge in the developing technology of covered-bridge building was the multiple kingpost, which features uprights with center-slanted braces along the sides of the bridge. *Swift River Bridge, Conway, New Hampshire*

OPPOSITE: Windows were optional on the original covered bridges across America, which were erected for functional reasons rather than for tourism or ornamentation. *Lancaster County, Pennsylvania*

eventually and naturally came to the point of Wernwag's bridge at Harpers Ferry, which occupied the most logical crossing point over the Potomac for many miles. But the existing bridge had been built for wagon, animal, and foot traffic, not for rail travel. Trains could not handle the existing sharp curves at the entrances to the bridge. To resolve the matter, Wernwag added new spans, with angles that trains could negotiate, at both existing entrances.

When the Winchester & Potomac Railroad decided to connect with the B&O at Harpers Ferry, it appeared that many historically important buildings stood in the way of progress. Again Wernwag came up with the solution. He simply added yet another

span and placed the juncture of the two railroad lines 125 feet out over the water of the river, right on the bridge.

The coming of the "iron horse" as the primary means of transport across America was both a major surge in covered-bridge building opportunity and a signal that the heyday of the wooden spans was coming to an end. As trains grew bigger and heavier the problems for wooden spans also became greater.

New design followed new design, usually solving the current situation temporarily but occasionally not proving itself in the move from drawing board to real life. Covered railroad bridges continued well into the 1930s, but with constantly decreasing numbers.

Some early American covered-bridge design elements, including arched floors, are incorporated into this relatively recent structure. *Jackson, New Hampshire*

OPPOSITE: Built in 1945 over the South Fork of the Santiam River in Oregon's Willamette Valley, Short Bridge is one of the newer wooden covered bridges in the country. *Linn County, Oregon*

CHAPTER THREE

A GEOGRAPHIC OVERVIEW

NEW ENGLAND

While the New England states may not live up to their image as leaders in the numbers of covered bridges still in existence, they certainly have—and had—an abundance of the spans. Many of the features of early barn architecture of the Yankee region can be seen in the covered bridges as well.

The saltbox roof, which features a longer "north" roof facing into the prevailing winds of the region, was common. Often the north roof stood partially over a special pedestrian walkway that was separated by trusswork from the wagon passageway. A particularly quaint and attractive example of the saltbox-type covered bridge, complete with its "sidewalk," which actually extended out beyond the supporting floor beams of the bridge proper in a suspended fashion, stood for many years near Brattleboro, Vermont. Small, almost corncrib-like, gable-roofed covered bridges also are common.

Although it was Pennsylvania that gave birth to the first covered bridges, the idea of covering for protection from the elements originated in New England. In 1785, when Enoch Hale built the first American bridge with jointed segments over the Connecticut River, he protected those joints by boxing them in with frames, sides, and rooflike weatherplates. The overall bridge itself, however, was left exposed to the weather.

New England also gave rise to a form of bridge even more unique than the covered span—the floating bridge. The only remaining example of this type of bridge today is across Colt's Pond at Brookfield,

The tiny covered bridge over the Pemigewasset River in New Hampshire is a case study in the simple functionality that first gave rise to the idea of covered bridges. *Franconia Notch State Park, New Hampshire*

Vermont. The current bridge is the sixth generation of floating bridge to span the pond. The original was built in 1810.

The 320 feet of the bridge rest atop nearly four hundred oak barrels floated in the pond and held together by chains. The special bridge was the town's solution to a crossing over the pond, which was too wide for a conventional, single-span bridge but featured too soft a bottom to allow the sinking of piers to accommodate multiple spans.

Given such creative but straightforward approaches to bridge problems, it's no wonder that many of the early covered-bridge pioneers in America originated in New England.

One of these men was Nicholas Powers, who first led the construction of a covered bridge at the age of just twenty-one years. The 130-foot-long span at Pittsford Mills, Vermont, serviced the community from 1837 to 1931. However, Powers was better known for his flamboyant approach to confronting his detractors, such as sitting at the center of his projects when the temporary shoring was removed from beneath the finished product to demonstrate his confidence in its soundness. He knew his construction techniques, and his new bridges never failed him.

When the railroads came onto the scene, the Yankee bridge builders were once again up to the task. Many of these "latter-day" covered bridges varied very little in appearance from their horse- and foot-traffic predecessors. However, some designers saw and seized the

OPPOSITE: Steel girders supporting portions of wooden covered bridges, particularly in East Coast states, generally represent repair and refurbishment attempts of more recent years. *Swiftwater Bridge, White Mountains, New Hampshire*

Many communities take great pride in their covered bridges and regularly proclaim their efforts to protect, maintain, and improve the bridge prominently on the bridges themselves. *White Mountain Covered Bridge, Albany, New Hampshire*

opportunity to come up with something that was noticeably new and different.

At Swanton, Vermont, the railroad bridge over the Missisquoi River reflected its creator's acknowledgment that something needed to be done with all the smoke that the iron-horse belched as it moved through the wooden "tunnel." The bridge stood very tall, relative to its one-track width, to collect the smoke in the rafters, and included three cupolas to vent it to the outside.

By contrast, the bridge that carried the early rails into Hartford, Connecticut, from 1816 to 1895, was very low and broad, accommodating two tracks across its span. Its many windows allowed train passengers quick glimpses of the riverscape as they clattered along the rails.

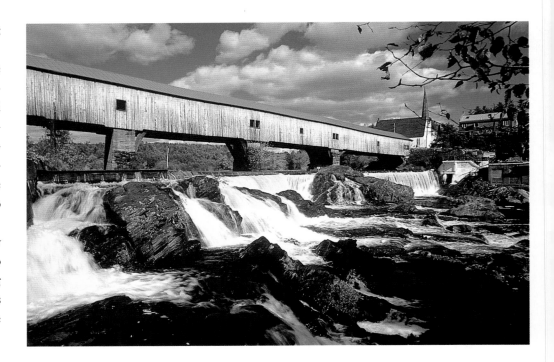

Examples of very long covered bridges, such as this four-span bridge across the Wild Ammonoosuc River, are very rare today. *Swiftwater Bridge, Bath, New Hampshire*

Still sturdy and sound after well over a century, this bridge is no longer used. The roadway for modern traffic has passed it by. *Baltimore Bridge No. 81, Springfield, Vermont*

OPPOSITE: Modern day meets yesteryear as bicycle racers in the Tour DuPont, clad in the latest spandex and riding supremely high-tech bikes, cross a New England covered bridge. *Jackson, New Hampshire*

THE EAST

With its relatively small streams, Delaware had no great need for elaborate covered bridges. Simple stringer bridges, or stone-foundation causeways, were adequate through most of the state. Several of Delaware's covered bridges were built in the 1820s by the famous Lewis Wernwag, incorporating his signature arch/kingpost design. Most of them crossed the Brandywine Creek into Pennsylvania.

Among the most notable of Delaware's covered bridges was the Summit Bridge over the Deep Cut gorge of the Chesapeake & Delaware Canal. Built in 1825 to span the mile-long man-made channel, complete with ornamental portals, the bridge continued in use until 1872 when it was replaced by a smaller, non-covered bridge.

Contrasting sharply with Delaware, the topography of Pennsylvania, with its large rivers and multitude of smaller streams, was primed for the benefits of the covered bridge. At one point in its history, nearly every county—sixty-five of sixty-seven—held at least one covered wooden span. Lancaster County boasted the greatest concentration, with thirty-seven at one point.

ABOVE: The steel wheels of the buggies and the shoes of the horses of the Amish can take a heavy toll on wooden bridge surfaces. In Amish country, many covered bridges have protective metal runners on their floor surfaces. *Lancaster County, Pennsylvania*

LEFT: Although many covered bridges near major battlefields of the Civil War were destroyed during the conflict, a few historic areas still hold some of the most abundant remaining supplies of covered bridges. *Gettysburg, Pennsylvania*

Although the old stone farmhouse that once stood by this covered bridge in Pennsylvania long ago fell into disrepair, local attention obviously has kept the bridge in a near-original condition. *Bridge No. 212, Haupt's Mill, Pennsylvania*

In addition to the first covered bridge, Pennsylvania had a half-stake in the first covered bridge to connect two states. Running from Trenton, New Jersey, to Morrisville, Pennsylvania, the 1,000-foot-long construction was completed on January 30, 1806, by Theodore Burr.

The state's history is filled with the tales of magnificent covered bridges, but a small span in Bedford County holds the trophy as most notorious. Although the Juniata Crossings bridge was built as a double-barrel (two passageways) in 1818, it was eventually cut back to a single-barrel bridge. The bridge portals featured a single wide opening, but several dozen feet inside a center truss divided the one lane into two. This worked well until automobiles became a common feature on the bridge. With the greater speeds of their vehicles, many drivers had close calls indeed with that center truss. Nevertheless, the bridge was kept in service until 1936 when an ice jam carried it in bits and pieces downstream.

If Pennsylvania should hold the title of "the covered-bridge state," then Lancaster County should be its capital. In the countryside to the east of the Susquehanna, away from the massive river-crossing bridges that were attracting national attention, builders erected some of the finest small covered bridges over streams and

Each suspended section of a bridge between supporting piers or shores is known as a span. Here we see a single-span bridge. *Uhlerstown Bridge, Bucks County, Pennsylvania*

Covered bridges were constructed over man-made waterways, such as canals, as well as natural streams and rivers. This bridge crosses an abandoned canal running along the Delaware River. *Uhlerstown Bridge, Bucks County, Pennsylvania*

49

Originally constructed in 1892 and rebuilt in 1979, this covered bridge in the Shenandoah Valley, with its Burr truss design, spans 204 feet. *Meems Bottom Bridge, Virginia*

creeks. Many of these original structures remain today, some with little additional work.

The Amish of Lancaster County—also known incorrectly as the Pennsylvania Dutch—still use these bridges daily. This can be hard on wooden bridges since the Amish religion prohibits the use of modern rubber tires. Instead, metal wheels with steel cleats are used on farm machinery and wood-with-iron wheels on horse-drawn buggies. For this reason, some of the covered bridges of Lancaster County have steel-plate runners along their floors.

While the construction of covered bridges was being fueled by Pennsylvania's western expansion, the first covered bridges in Maryland found their beginnings in that state's need for connection to the east, across the wide expanses of the lower Susquehanna River. The ever-busy Theodore Burr, already engaged beyond his capacities on three projects upriver in Pennsylvania, was asked to expand his responsibilities to include the first of Maryland's covered bridges.

At Rock Run from 1817 to 1819, Burr employed three islands and eighteen 200-foot-long spans to erect a covered bridge of 4,170 feet, the first non-ferry crossing of the Susquehanna into Maryland. About half of Burr's work was lost in 1823, when sparks from the metal runners of a sleigh ignited a wagonload of hay,

Maintenance is a constant need with wooden structures exposed to the elements. Although someone seems to be caring for this bridge, we still can see the marks of wear and tear. *Erwinna Bridge, Bucks County, Pennsylvania*

which in turn kindled the eastern half of the bridge. The timbers to rebuild the bridge were floated downstream from Lewis Wernwag's sawmill, upriver at Conowingo.

The bridge continued in service until 1854, when a panicked herd of cattle thundered through its rotting floor. In 1857 an ice jam finished the job.

The coastal and eastern regions of Virginia had no need for covered bridges, but across the Blue Ridge Mountains dividing the state there was another story. Although many were lost during the Civil War, more than a hundred covered bridges were built there.

Virginia's oldest covered bridge is also a span of unique design. Built in 1835 near Covington, Virginia, the Humpback Bridge employs several kingpost trusses along its sides in connection with upward arching beams for the roof and the floor. The bridge is the only one of three humpbacks built near Covington that year that remains today. One was burned by troops during the Civil War, and the second was torn away by flood.

The Deep South, owing to its geography and more temperate climate, never had as many covered bridges as states like Pennsylvania or Ohio. Some of the few built before the Civil War were reduced to ashes by the end of that tragic conflict.

As in other regions of the country, the architecture of the South's covered bridges often copied that of its barns. Thus, we see the top-hat roof design and long, tall, narrow constructions on bridges that were common in the tobacco barns.

LEFT: **Built in 1904 with many spans resting on huge stone piers, this Alabama covered bridge is the largest in the region.** *Clarkson Bridge, Alabama*

OPPOSITE: **Most of the smaller covered bridges across the country were built by local carpenters, who copied the larger spans of the more famous builders but also brought their own ideas into the process.** *Lake Lauralee Bridge, Sterrett, Alabama*

THE MIDDLE WEST

As the nation expanded westward, the designs of eastern covered bridges traveled with the pioneering settlers. Although much of the continent was suited to stone bridges due to scarcity of trees and abundance of stone, eastern-style spans were erected where conditions were favorable. The influence of Pennsylvania, Maryland, and Virginia can be seen clearly in the covered bridges that remain as far west as Oregon and Washington state.

Although not a state immediately associated with the Civil War, Ohio lost some of its covered bridges during that struggle to Confederate forces led north out of Tennessee by General John Hunt Morgan. His raiders torched bridges at Bergholz, Dunkinsville, Lore City, and Point Pleasant. In addition, defenders at a covered bridge near Paint Creek skittishly sparked a fire on a bridge they were defending when it was rumored that Morgan's forces were nearby.

Weather and time have taken a much greater toll on the Buckeye State's covered bridges. About forty of the state's counties have at least one surviving span. Columbiana County, in the southeastern portion of the state, is typical. While once there were more than a hundred covered bridges within its borders, today there are but a half-dozen. Fairfield County is atypical, with thirty covered bridges remaining, the second-highest total of any county in the United States.

The longest of Ohio's remaining covered bridges is the Harpersfield Bridge, crossing 236 feet of the Grand River in two spans. Also unique in Ohio is the Newton Falls bridge over the East Branch of the Mahoning River, the only one in the state that includes an extra, covered sidewalk for pedestrians. The Humpback in Vinton County is notable for the 19-inch arch, top and bottom. And, of course, there is the Jonathan Bright No. 2 Bridge at Carroll, which is both a covered bridge and a supension bridge with metal supports.

As Indiana was hurrying to develop its transportation system and connect into the growing national roadway network, state-funded projects pushed along the first covered bridges in the Hoosier State. The very first of these, just a short 49-footer, was built across Symons Creek near Straughn in 1831.

New wood siding, modern steel supports, and constant maintenance will guarantee a long life for this single-span bridge built around 1850. Barrett's Mill Bridge, Highland County, Ohio.

OPPOSITE: During the Civil War the destruction brought by Morgan's Raiders included the burning of two covered bridges crossing Ohio's White Oak Creek. Today's surviving bridge in this area dates from 1895. *New Hope Bridge, Brown County, Ohio*

FOLLOWING PAGE: The tight lattice-type trusswork of the Ithiel Town design allows for uncovered openings in the bridge sides with minimal exposure for the interior lumber. *Vicinity of Buckeye Lake State Park, Ohio*

MCBRIDE BRIDGE
BUILT 1871

A few decades and many covered bridges later, one of Indiana's greatest covered-bridge builders, J. J. Daniels, came onto the scene. Through the end of the century, he directed the construction of more than fifty spans, both for roadway and rail. The Kennedy family, three generations beginning with Archibald Michael Kennedy, contributed a like number to the state, each exhibiting the fine finish and trim that the artisan family insisted upon.

In Parke County, its three dozen covered bridges are the focus of an annual Covered Bridge Festival held for ten days each year since October 1957. Such is the sentiment in this rural county for the bridges that a covered bridge "living" museum was established in 1968.

ABOVE: Parke County, Indiana, is noted for its store of covered bridges. Each summer it becomes a mecca for enthusiasts who attend the annual Covered Bridge Festival. A highlight for visitors is Mansfield Bridge, built around 1867 by Joseph J. Daniels. *Mansfield, Indiana*

LEFT: A modern concrete bridge now carries traffic across Sugar Creek in Indiana. The old covered bridge it has supplanted remains, but is used only by pedestrians. *Narrows Bridge, Turkey Run State Park, Indiana*

OPPOSITE: Flat roofs, with their inherent problems in diverting rainfall and snow, were a relatively rare feature among covered bridges. *McBride Bridge, Madison County, Iowa*

As the redbud blooms in spring, the wear and tear of many winters is apparent on the weathered and broken sides of this covered bridge. *Cataract Falls State Park, Indiana*

Compared to most other bridge-roof designs, these are nearly flat. The bridges inspire the community pride necessary to maintain and safeguard them.

None of the Madison County bridges, however, is the oldest in Iowa. That honor goes to a small bridge erected in 1869 across the North Fork of Skunk River near the town of Delta. With a few modern additions for support, it has stood the test of time.

The elements, fire, and need for more modern spans have been hard on the covered bridges of Michigan. Of the remaining seven—all grouped within a few miles of Grand Rapids— two are rebuilt replicas of predecessors lost to fire. Another, the Ackley bridge, is a transplant from Pennsylvania into the museum-park, Greenfield Village, in Dearborn.

Covered bridges in Iowa can mostly be found in Madison County, which gave title to the bestseller, *The Bridges of Madison County.* Seven of the twelve remaining covered bridges in Iowa are located there. All are of the Town design, with five featuring the unique innovation of roofs with very little pitch.

The oldest covered bridge in the state, built in 1862, stands in Fallasburg Park. The youngest, built in 1980, is a replica of an 1866 bridge and is found in a community park in Ada.

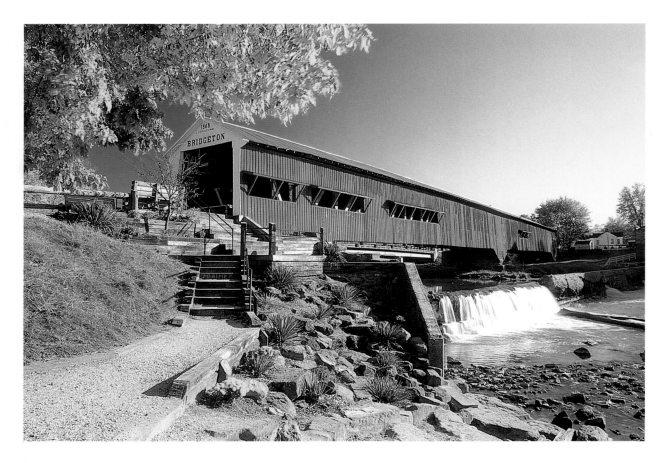

This two-span covered bridge has stood the test of time. Built in 1868, the bridge enjoys strong support from the community and has been maintained in mint condition. *Bridgeton, Parke County, Indiana*

OPPOSITE: In a relatively rare design feature, the lower ends of the truss timbers extend through the bottom of the bridge. *Fallasburg, Michigan*

THE PACIFIC STATES

Although covered bridges are not part of the popular western image, they were very important to the Old West. Beginning in 1850, one year after the famous Gold Rush, more than 1,000 covered bridges were eventually built west of the Rocky Mountains. Bridges in Arizona, Nevada, Idaho, and Montana crossed water barriers and provided vital commercial links between growing western communities. Today, however, the only surviving covered bridges in the West are found in California, Oregon, and Washington.

Wood was abundant in the Pacific Northwest, and it was wood of species well-suited for the strenuous duties of bridge timbers. The famous redwood of northern California was a natural choice, as was the Douglas fir in timber-rich Oregon and Washington. The latter was also sought after for bridge projects far to the east. But in these western states the timbers often came from the immediate vicinity of the bridge site itself.

Although many eastern designs and techniques were used by western builders, it was the work of Massachusetts-born William Howe that was perhaps most influential. He designed the first successful combination of wood and metal in a single truss in a way that was durable and economical. Though lacking the picturesque lines of eastern bridges, Howe's simple,

In some locations, local sentiment favored keeping the traditional covered bridge but adapting it to new needs. The original, one-lane bridge over Sheep Pen Creek in California was replaced with a two-laner in the early 1970s. *Jedediah Smith Redwoods State Park, California*

The only covered bridge still in use in Washington state demonstrates an unusual, rounded variation of the gable-on-hip style of roofing much more common on barns. *Grays River Valley, Washington*

Bridges such as this in the Pacific Northwest often feature the special ornamentation that some of the earlier covered-bridge builders in the East incorporated into their designs. *Goodpasture Bridge, Vida, Oregon*

for several decades beginning in the 1870s.

At one time in the early 1900s, there were more than 450 covered bridges in Oregon, but despite continued new construction into the 1960s, today fewer than fifty remain. All are west of the Cascades, and all but one are maintained by counties or private owners.

Between 1910 and World War II, nearly eight covered bridges disappeared from Oregon each year to accommodate more modern means of transportation. The trend slowed in the late 1950s, when most road construction was devoted to new interstate highways rather than to replacement of existing secondary roadways and their bridges.

In more recent years, covered bridges have either been replaced by new covered spans or left standing with roadways re-routed around them.

unadorned structures were the cheapest way to span waterways and were widely accepted.

A. S. Miller & Sons were another force in bridge-building, with their exclusive Pacific Coast rights to the truss design of Ohio's Robert W. Smith. Their all-wood bridges were the most popular in the West

LEFT: Some bridges, which combine the ideas of both the multiple kingpost style of truss and the Long truss, are now relocated in historic parks and outdoor museums. *Weddle Bridge, Sankey Park, Sweet Home, Oregon*

OPPOSITE: Built as recently as 1920, this is the last covered bridge still in use on the Pacific Highway. *Grave Creek, Josephine County, Oregon*

DONAHOE BRIDGE
BUILT 1870

CHAPTER FOUR

THE LORE OF COVERED BRIDGES

Unlike most modern bridges, which take the route numbers of the highways that cross them, the covered bridges generally attracted specific names that revealed something special about them. The name of the farm family that lived nearest the bridge and owned the land on which the bridge rested, at least at one end, was a common source of identification. The names of nearby towns sometimes came to apply to the bridges as well, although the bridge often preceded the town and was not located in it. Or perhaps the bridge had some unique characteristic associated with its appearance or history that seemed to fit as a name.

GHOST STORIES

Covered bridges have given rise to more than their fair share of localized folklore and legend. Ghost stories, usually connected with someone alleged to have lost his or her life on or near the bridge, are particularly common. They often include some reason for the ghost to occasionally appear to users of the bridge, such as asking for the person's head or something else of value.

These imposing structures did attract their share of death, for both man and beast, on rare occasions because of collapse but much more often due to reasons only

Covered bridges, along with white steeples and snowy landscapes, have long been part of American holiday imagery. Waitfield, Vermont

RIGHT: The romance of covered bridges is not frozen in the past. A recent novel places a modern-day love story around a bridge such as this one. McBride Bridge, Madison County, Iowa

OPPOSITE: Red and white, both separately and in combination, are the traditional covered-bridge colors, as they are the traditional colors of paint for barns and similar architectural features on the early American landscape. Cutler-Donahoe Bridge, Winterset, Iowa

Unlike most modern spans, covered bridges seem to blend into their environments with little intrusion on the natural landscape. *Passaconway Bridge, White Mountains, New Hampshire*

Romantic spots in all seasons, covered bridges became known as "kissing bridges." Young couples in buggies crossed them more slowly than necessary or used them as rendezvous points. *Grafton, Vermont*

OPPOSITE: Far from towns or villages, even a small covered bridge could serve as a gathering place for christenings, weddings, funerals, and meetings of all kinds. *Grafton, Vermont*

indirectly connected to the soundness of the bridge.

Such was the case of a suicide on the bridge for the Lebanon & Tremont (later the Reading) Railroad at Westmont Station, one of the few covered bridges built to carry a roadway over railroad tracks. A down-on-his-luck man hung himself from the floor timbers of the roadway, which left his body dangling above the railroad tracks. Travelers on the windowless, bright-yellow, covered bridge were unaware of the tragedy just beneath their feet, until the engineer of the next train to pass spotted the horrible scene in his headlight.

Some of this lore included privileges for more fortunate travelers. Many people in covered-bridge country refer to the spans offhandedly as "kissing bridges" in reference to the tradition that when a young couple was courting, the man was supposedly entitled to a buss from his sweetheart as their wagon or buggy passed across the bridge. "Wishing bridges" are another common reference, again referring to the granting of a favor to anyone who made a wish while using the bridge. Well into the 1800s, many covered bridges were operated as toll-crossings. This situation gave rise to many special rules that today seem strange. For example, tollkeepers charged additional amounts from those who ran their horses across the bridges, to compensate for the additional damages that pound-

As light fades and a darkened bridge lies ahead, one can sense the inspiration behind such ghostly tales as Washington Irving's "The Legend of Sleepy Hollow." *Woodstock, Vermont*

RIGHT: A fresh winter snowfall gains additional splendor when viewed through the window of a covered bridge where weathered timbers frame an almost magical scene. *Hillsborough County, New Hampshire*

OPPOSITE: Strange sounds, such as wind whistling through their timbers, as well as suicides or murders, could cause some bridges to be avoided, even in broad daylight. *East Randolph, Vermont*

FOLLOWING PAGE: A bridge, sturdily built of wood and stone and matching the beauty of the land, can aptly be called "a poem stretched across a river." *Hillsborough County, New Hampshire*

ing hooves could do to the wooden floors. Different rates often were charged for animals that crossed the bridges on wagons, rather than pulling them, for this same reason. And, when traveling circuses were a regular feature of the American landscape, elephants often were charged at a special rate just for their bulk. Sometimes they were even excluded from use of the span.

MORE THAN PASSAGE

Covered bridges have also been put to many wide-ranging, non-travel uses over the years. Today, about the only such use that continues to any extent is as photographic background. Throughout covered-bridge areas in all parts of America, wedding photographers have found that the curving, arching shapes of the old spans make wondrous settings for pictures of that special day.

In ages past, when large public facilities were at a premium in American small towns and in the countryside, the relatively substantial amounts of shel-

tered floor space on a covered bridge attracted many public meetings, for both community and church. Less attractively, lynch mobs also found the bridges to be satisfactory gathering and planning places.

Local troops of soldiers regularly trained under the protection of covered bridges before marching off to the Civil War. Some skirmishes in

ABOVE: The unprotected, often out-of-the-way timbers of covered bridges have become a regular target of graffiti artists, who show no respect for the architectural concepts that went into the massive timbers. *Holliwell Bridge, Madison County, Iowa*

RIGHT: Whether for picnicking, fishing, or swimming, covered bridges have long been the focus for many of summer's greatest pleasures. *North Hartland, Vermont*

OPPOSITE: The spirit of community that seems to surround our remaining covered bridges expresses itself in many ways, from mint-condition maintenance to Yuletide decorations. *Swiftwater Bridge, White Mountains, New Hampshire*

The antique car and the covered bridge seem likely companions in our historical sense, but the coming of the automobile actually signaled the end of the glory days of the covered bridge. *Cornish-Windsor Bridge, Cornish, New Hampshire*

Covered bridges and farming country generally go hand-in-hand. One never knows what errant species of barnyard livestock might be encountered on these spans. *Bucks County, Pennsylvania*

that great conflagration even centered around the bridges.

For example, Sauk's Bridge, built over Marsh Creek southwest of Gettysburg in 1854, saw heavy use by all sorts of military vehicles and troops by both the Union and Confederate armies throughout that famous battle. Why some officer of one side or the other did not order it burned, as was a common practice during the Civil War, remains a mystery. Travelers can still enjoy the bridge near Eisenhower Farm.

The relatively large sides of covered bridges and the ready audiences provided at their openings attracted those with a message to tell, or sell. "Prepare To Meet Thy Lord" and "Repent" can still be found on many a covered bridge, sometimes in faded lettering, sometimes in a newly applied coat of paint. Some bridges have even taken on the name of some advertising that had been painted on their sides. Such was the case with the "Wizard Oil Bridge" in Ohio, until the wooden bridge was replaced by a steel span earlier this century.

On the down side of this aspect of covered bridges, graffiti "artists" have found the wooden structures to be easy targets for their offending carvings. In the modern world, four-letter attacks have become common, spoiling many a vacationer's photo recollections with something they missed when they took the shot. Given the isolated locations of many covered bridges, little can be done on an ongoing basis to thwart these attacks.

A DWINDLING RESOURCE

The count seems to drop a few each year; the current U.S. leader in number of covered bridges is Pennsylvania, followed by Ohio, Indiana, Oregon, and Vermont. Others among the thirty-three states with healthy shares of the less than sixteen hundred covered bridges that still remain across America are Alabama, California, Kentucky, New Hampshire, New York, and West Virginia.

Although many of us are surprised to learn this fact— Vermont is often the first guess as the leader in covered bridges—this is changing as the "word" on covered bridges is getting out through various covered-bridge celebrations and annual tours. Nearly every county or region with more than a half-dozen covered bridges has joined in this ongoing tourism craze.

The renewed interest in covered bridges, for tourism and for other reasons, has been good for the old wooden spans. Many that had fallen into disrepair have been brought back to life through community-based projects. Others that had been victimized by arsonists— like barns, covered bridges are big, isolated, and

ABOVE: Used for traffic until 1962, this span north of Milwaukee is Wisconsin's last authentic covered bridge. *Cedarburg, Wisconsin*

LEFT: The stream areas under covered bridges are special places to explore, swim, and just relax on a hot summer afternoon. *West Dummerstone Bridge, Vermont*

RIGHT: The reflection of a covered bridge in the waterway it crosses seems to be a portal through time into a quieter, more peaceful, less hectic period in America's history. *Uhlerstown Bridge, Bucks County, Pennsylvania*

attractive targets—have subsequently been the recipients of outpourings of local support.

Still other examples that would have gone the way of the wrecking crew have been salvaged, and even restored, right next to the concrete or steel spans that replaced them, or moved into nearby parks. The record holder for such migration goes to the Ackley Bridge, which was built in 1832 to span the Enslow Fork of Wheeling Creek on the Greene-Washington county line in Pennsylvania.

By 1937 it had fallen far into disrepair, when agents of Henry Ford—sent out to locate an authentic covered bridge for the industrialist's historic Greenfield Village in Dearborn, Michigan—spotted it and arranged for its dismantling and transfer. It now stands over a manmade stream almost 300 miles west of its original location, restored to mint condition.

This is not to say that all of America's remaining covered bridges are now in close-to-original condition. Far too many have found no public sentiment to tap, or at least insufficient public sentiment. They stand off to the side in forgotten, out-of-the-way locations, slowly falling bit by bit into the waters they cross.

A timed photographic exposure creates a surreal effect as evening traffic emerges from a lighted covered bridge. *West Cornwall, Connecticut*

OPPOSITE: Nearly all the covered bridges still in use today service secondary roads with limited traffic. Some have been closed to traffic and left in place while supplanted by a newer span nearby. *Uhlerstown Bridge, Bucks County, Pennsylvania*

PHOTO CREDITS

Photographer/Page Number

American Landscapes
Ray Atkeson 62-63
Rick Schafer 16, 38, 64 (bottom), 65

Pat Anderson 13 (top & bottom), 34 (bottom), 75 (top)

Scott Arnold 19 (top), 44 (top)

Bullaty Lomeo 4, 11 (top & bottom), 18 (top), 27 (top), 28 (top), 43, 49 (top & bottom), 51, 76 (bottom), 78 (top), 79

Ed Cooper 58, 61, 66, 67 (bottom)

Kent and Donna Dannen 32, 50, 52, 53, 54, 55, 56-57, 59 (top & bottom), 63 (right)

Dembinsky Photo Associates
Dan Dempster 39
Terry Donnelly 35 (bottom)
Dusty Perin 36
Stephen J. Shaluta 31

Dan Dempster 60 (bottom)

Jack A. Keller 21, 24-25, 30, 64 (top)

Patti McConville 37, 77 (top)

Joe McDonald 47 (right)

New England Stock Photo
Thomas W. Chase 26
Peter Cole 68 (top)
Brooks Dodge 33, 45
Fred M. Dole 5, 8-9, 18 (bottom), 23 (top), 67 (top), 69, 74
Martin E. Harwood 17 (top), 68 (bottom)
Bill Lea 20
Effin Older 76 (top)
Margo Taussig Pinkerton 17 (bottom), 23 (bottom), 29 (bottom) 44 (bottom)
H. Schmeiser 19 (bottom)
Jim Schwabel 14, 29 (top)
Clyde H. Smith 12, 48, 75 (bottom)

Picture Perfect, USA
Dodie Miller 70
John Warden 15, 28 (bottom)
Brian Yarvin 10, 78 (bottom)

James P. Rowan 6, 34 (top), 35 (top)

Stephen R. Swinburne 17, 27 (bottom), 71 (top), 77 (bottom)

Tom Till 22, 40-41, 42, 46-47, 60 (top), 71 (bottom), 72-73